CONTE

D1632712

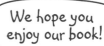

We hope you enjoy our book!

INTRODUCTION

When people say '**The City of London**', they are referring to a tiny borough in the heart of the London metropolis. It's about one mile from west to east and one mile from north to south – that's why we call it 'The Square Mile'!

The City is unique. It has its own Lord Mayor, its own police force and its own parliament, which is called the Court of Common Council. The City's boundaries are marked by dragons, holding shields with the City's emblem.

During the working day, the City has a population of about 350,000 people. Many of them work at banks, insurance companies and other financial institutions. When the working day is done, however, the population shrinks dramatically! Fewer than 10,000 people actually reside within the City.

Dragon Monuments
mark the City boundaries.

The City is an ancient and historic part of London, which was settled by the Romans in approximately Year 43. With nearly two thousand years of history to explore, it's difficult to know where to begin – and where to end! Every building, every street and every cobblestone is filled with its own history, so we had to make some difficult editorial choices when we created this book. After all, we wanted to leave space for puzzle pages at the back!

In our exploration of the City, we started with ancient maps. We looked at them closely, and we compared them to other maps throughout history. We saw for ourselves how the City has developed and changed.

What we discovered, above all, is that the City has always been a place for work and business. And with so much history, it is a place which has a rich sense of ceremony and tradition.

Our book features the institutions which have played a central role in City life: Mansion House, Guildhall, the Old Bailey, the Royal Exchange, St Paul's Cathedral and the Bank of England.

You'll read about these and other landmarks in this book. But the best way to learn about them is to visit them! It's all right there, within a square mile, for you to discover for yourself.

Enjoy!

Guy Fox

The Bowler Hat
If you walk through the City, you may see a business man wearing a bowler hat. Bowler hats were popular in the City in the late 19th and early 20th century.

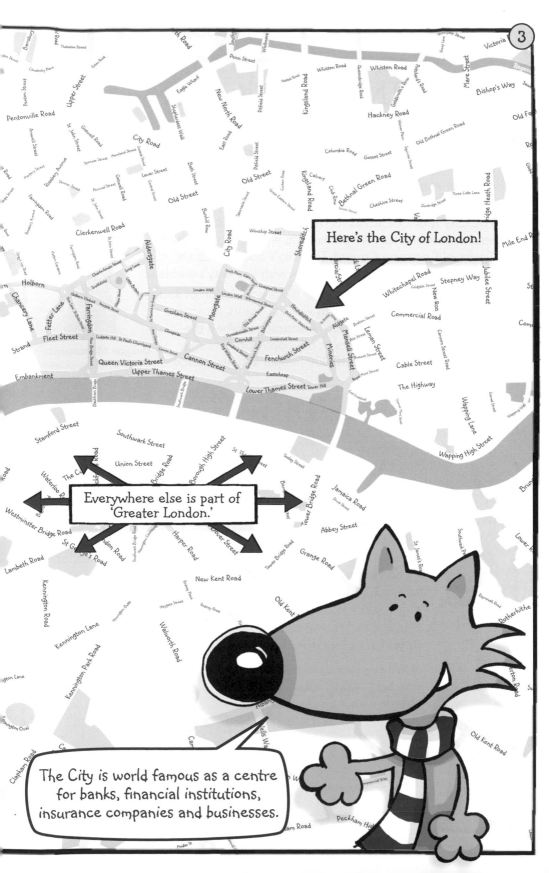

Here's the City of London!

Everywhere else is part of 'Greater London.'

The City is world famous as a centre for banks, financial institutions, insurance companies and businesses.

CITY MAP

Cock Lane
Giltspur Street
London Wall
Basinghall
Noble Street
Oat Lane
Love Lane
Aldermanbury
Basinghall Street
Wood Street

Court
Newgate Street
Angel Street
Guildhall

ane
The Old Bailey
Gresham Street
Gresham Str

Old Bailey
Warwick Lane
Amen Court
Carey Lane
Foster Lane
Gutter Lane
Wood Street
Milk Street
Mumford Court
Russia Row
King Street
Ironmonger Lane
Old Jewry

Paternoster Row
Cheapside
Dove Court
Poultry

St Paul's

Igrim Street
Carter Lane
Creed Lane
Dean's Court
Carter Lane
Godliman Street
St Paul's Cathedral
New Change
Bread Street
Queen Street
Queen Victoria Street

Addle Street
Knightrider Street
Watling Street

Queen Victoria Street
Distaff Lane
Friday Street
Cannon Street
Cannon Street

Puddle Dock
Lamb Street
Little Trinity Lane
Garlick Hill
Mansion House
Queen Street
Cloak Lane
College Hill
Scor

Up   es Street
College Street

> In the Middle Ages, they built a wall around the City. The area encircled by that wall, more or less, remains the boundary of the City.

Southwark Brid
All Hall

There are no 'Roads' within the City!

But there are plenty of streets and alleys, and a lot of them have interesting names. Many of them were named after the trades which were practiced there. Some are named after foods, like 'Milk Street', and others are named after jobs, like 'Ironmonger Lane'. If you look closely, you'll find lots of them!

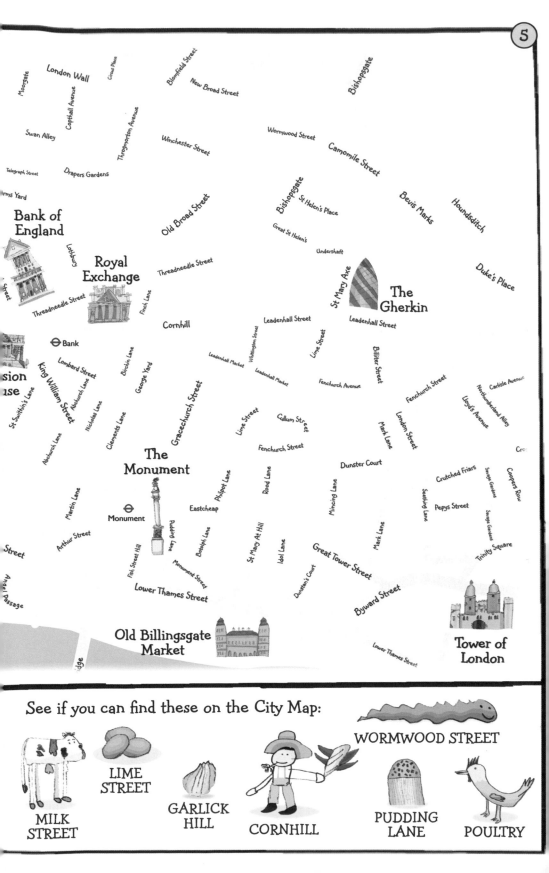

Moorgate
London Wall
Circus Place
Blomfield Street
New Broad Street
Bishopsgate
Copthall Avenue
Throgmorton Avenue
Winchester Street
Wormwood Street
Camomile Street
Swan Alley
Telegraph Street
Drapers Gardens
rms Yard
Bishopsgate
St Helen's Place
Bevis Marks
Houndsditch

Bank of England
Old Broad Street
Great St Helen's
Lothbury
Royal Exchange
Threadneedle Street
Undershaft
Duke's Place

St Mary Axe
The Gherkin
Threadneedle Street
Finch Lane
Cornhill
Leadenhall Street
Leadenhall Street
Street

Bank
Lombard Street
Birchin Lane
George Yard
Leadenhall Market
Washington Street
Lime Street
Billiter Street
Fenchurch Street
Carlisle Avenue
sion
se
King William Street
Abchurch Lane
Nicholas Lane
Leadenhall Market
Fenchurch Avenue
Lloyd's Avenue
Northumberland Alley

St Swithin's Lane
Clements Lane
Gracechurch Street
Lime Street
Cullum Street
Mark Lane
London Street
Abchurch Lane
The Monument
Fenchurch Street
Dunster Court
Crutched Friars
Savage Gardens
Coopers Row
Cro

Martin Lane
Monument
Philpot Lane
Rood Lane
Mincing Lane
Seething Lane
Pepys Street
Savage Gardens

Street
Arthur Street
Eastcheap
Pudding Lane
Botolph Lane
St Mary At Hill
Idol Lane
Great Tower Street
Mark Lane
Trinity Square

Angel Passage
Fish Street Hill
Monument Street
Dunstan's Court
Byward Street

Lower Thames Street
Lower Thames Street
Tower of London

dge
Old Billingsgate Market

See if you can find these on the City Map:

WORMWOOD STREET

LIME STREET

GARLICK HILL

MILK STREET

CORNHILL

PUDDING LANE

POULTRY

WELCOME TO THE CITY!

MEET THE LORD MAYOR

The 'Right Honourable Lord Mayor of London' is 'first citizen' of the City and the Head of the City of London. He or she also serves as an ambassador and promotes the businesses and institutions which are located in the City.

Henry Fitz-Ailwyn, First Mayor of the City.
Engraved by W. Woodcock in 1850.
Published with the kind permission of the London Metropolitan Archives.

> As Lord Mayor, I serve only the City of London! Don't confuse me with the Mayor of London, who serves <u>all</u> of London.

In 1189, Henry Fitz-Ailwyn was the first mayor. Since then 682 people, including Dick Whittington, have had the job.

The Lord Mayor serves a term of one year, and the job is unpaid!

Each November, the current Lord Mayor passes the ceremonial sword, mace and purse to the new Lord Mayor. The completely silent ceremony takes place at Guildhall and is called the 'Silent Change'.

On the next day, the Lord Mayor travels in a golden horse-drawn coach from Guildhall to the Royal Courts of Justice to swear allegiance to the monarch. It's called 'The Lord Mayor's Show' and it is one of London's oldest annual events.

DID YOU KNOW?
The Lord Mayor's coach had no brakes until 1851!

Anonymous etching of the **Lord Mayor's Procession**, from 1840.
Published with the kind permission of the London Metropolitan Archives.

Royal Standard & Banners   *Trumpeters*   *Union Jack*   *Guar...*

MANSION HOUSE

- Is the office and home of the Lord Mayor during the one-year term of office.

- Designed by George Dance the Elder and completed in 1753.

- Sir Crispin Gascoigne, who was Lord Mayor in 1752, was so eager to live there, he actually moved in before it was finished!

- Inside, there is a banqueting hall called the 'Egyptian Hall' where the Lord Mayor holds grand events.

- The building has jail cells for prisoners, which were used when the building served as the Lord Mayor's magistrate court.

- One jail cell, 'The Birdcage,' was used for ladies only, and suffragette Emmeline Pankhurst spent time there.

- The Mansion House also has an amazing collection of Dutch paintings!

VISITOR INFORMATION:
Guided Tour: Available every Tuesday at 2:00 PM (Arrive at 1:45 PM).
Please check the website for changes to the schedule.
Cost: £6 for Adults   Tube Station: Bank
Website: http://tinyurl.com/VisitMansionHouse
For more details on the Lord Mayor's Show: www.lordmayorsshow.org

LEARN HOW TO DRAW IT!
Download a free 'How to Draw Mansion House' lesson at www.guyfox.org.uk.

Lord Mayor

Guy Fox presents...

A HISTORY OF THE CITY

THE ROMANS

In about 43 AD, the Romans built a settlement near the River Thames which was called 'Londinium.' They chose that particular place for two reasons: First, the river was deep enough for big ships. Second, it was narrow enough to build a bridge across it.

And build they did! The Romans built the first London Bridge in about 50 AD, and they didn't stop there. They built roads and temples and amphitheatres and palaces and warehouses along the river. And, after Boudicca's army burned everything to the ground, the Romans built it all over again.

Londinium became the capital of Roman Britain. It was an important centre for trade and government.

> Some people call me 'Boadicea'. In Welsh, my name is 'Buddug'.

Meet Boudicca...
(Around AD 30 to around AD 61)

Boudicca was the wife of Prasutagus, who was the chief of the Iceni tribe. When he died, the Romans took all the property of the tribal leaders and tried to rule the Iceni themselves. Even worse, they physically punished Boudicca, and they were cruel to her daughters.

So Boudicca organised a revolt against the Romans. Her army defeated the Romans at Colchester and burned it to the ground. Then they marched to Londinium, destroying it completely. The Romans finally defeated Boudicca in a battle near Verulamium (modern day St Albans). Legend has it, she poisoned herself before the Romans could kill her.

Timeline

Year 43 (approximately)
The Romans settle in 'Londinium'.

Londinium was a cultured and cosmopolitan city. Ships from across Europe sailed up the River Thames and offloaded their cargos to markets located there.

Between 180 and 220 AD, the Romans built a wall to protect Londinium from attack. Even now, you can see bits of this Roman Wall near the Tower of London and also at St Alphage's Garden.

Around Year 410, Emperor Honorius told citizens of Londinium that he could no longer defend them, so the Romans abandoned Londinium. For about one hundred and fifty years after that, we don't really know what happened in the City.

THE SAXONS & THE VIKINGS

We do know, in the 6th century, that Saxons from various places settled in areas around the deserted City. They preferred to live outside the walls where there was more land for their farms. Their settlement, which was a little bit west of the present-day City, was called 'Lundenwic'.

Under the Saxons, Lundenwic prospered and grew. It wasn't long before it gained the attention of the Danes who wanted 'Lundenburgh' for their own.

In 842, Danish Vikings attacked the Saxons, and they attacked again and again over the next two centuries. In 851, the Vikings rowed up the River Thames in their long boats and burned 'Lundenburgh' to the ground!

DID YOU KNOW? 'Alderman' comes from the Saxon word 'ealdorman'. An 'ealdorman' was the chief citizen in each ward; his job was to resolve arguments and to be neighbourhood commander in times of war.

We called the City 'Lundenwic'.

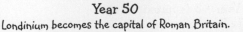

Year 50
Londinium becomes the capital of Roman Britain.

Year 60
Queen Boudicca leads a revolt!

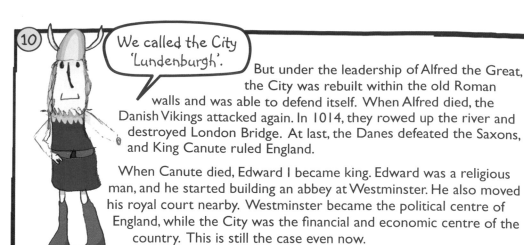

We called the City 'Lundenburgh'.

But under the leadership of Alfred the Great, the City was rebuilt within the old Roman walls and was able to defend itself. When Alfred died, the Danish Vikings attacked again. In 1014, they rowed up the river and destroyed London Bridge. At last, the Danes defeated the Saxons, and King Canute ruled England.

When Canute died, Edward I became king. Edward was a religious man, and he started building an abbey at Westminster. He also moved his royal court nearby. Westminster became the political centre of England, while the City was the financial and economic centre of the country. This is still the case even now.

THE NORMANS

Shortly after Westminster Abbey was finished, Edward died and was buried there. In 1066, William of Normandy invaded England and marched toward London. As a warning to the City, he burnt the area just south of the river (which is now called Southwark). The City welcomed William without a fight.

William made a peace deal with the City, granting its citizens the same rights which they had been granted under King Edward I.

DID YOU KNOW? Viking helmets did NOT have horns on them!
We apologise for the inaccuracy, but we think these drawings are FANTASTIC just the way they are!

Around 400
The Romans leave. The City falls into a 'Dark Age'.

6th Century
The Saxons settle just outside the City.

At the time of William's conquest, the City was already a well-established port and international marketplace. Wool was England's main export, with a thriving trade between City merchants and the clothmakers in northern Italy and in Flanders.

William was smart. He wanted City merchants to grow and prosper, because a prosperous City meant more tax money for his royal purse. But he didn't want City merchants to grow more powerful than himself.

William needed a permanent symbol of his power. And he needed a place to live! So he built the Tower of London, just outside the City borders, where he could keep an eye on everything that happened there.

THE CITY's RIGHTS

After William died in 1100, the kings who followed him needed the support of rich and powerful City merchants.

So they granted more rights to the City, including the right to collect taxes and to elect a sheriff. In 1189, Richard I allowed the City to elect its own mayor, and Henry Fitz-Ailwyn was the first person to hold the post.

In 1215, when John I signed the *Magna Carta*, all of the City's special rights were confirmed in writing. The City of London has enjoyed a unique status ever since.

DID YOU KNOW? The Magna Carta states, 'The City of London shall have all its ancient liberties and free customs....' This statement confirms the City's rights and its special status.

TOWER of LONDON

- Built by William I in the late 11th century to intimidate Londoners. He died before the 'White Tower' was completed.

- Located just outside the City.

- Has served as a royal palace, fortress, armoury, prison, mint, concert venue, ice rink and a menagerie.

- Henry III kept an elephant there!

VISITOR INFORMATION:
Open every day. Ticket prices vary.
Telephone: 0844 482 7799
Tube Station: Tower Hill or
                Tower Gateway
Website: www.hrp.org.uk/toweroflondon

I think I'll write a song about this!

840s to 994
The Danes make attacks on Lundenwic.

1014
Viking raiders pull down London Bridge!

With their rights firmly in place, merchants, tradesmen and craftsmen in the City could get on with what they did best: Making Money!

Gog & Magog, legendary giants, are the guardians of the City of London.

GUILDHALL

Since the 12th century, Guildhall has been the home of the City's government. It houses the City's parliament, administration offices, a library, a bookshop and an art gallery. There is also a magnificent hall where banquets and events are held.

THE OLD BAILEY

Criminals and debtors from the City were sent to Newgate Prison, located in a street called 'Old Bailey.' It was a horrid, dirty place. In 1423, Lord Mayor Richard Whittington (yes, the one from the pantomime) gave money to make it better and to add courts for criminal trials. Newgate Prison was eventually destroyed and a new court building was built there. Nowadays, the 'Old Bailey' is the nickname for the Central Criminal Courts, and criminal trials are held there.

GUILDHALL

- The ceremonial and administrative home of the City of London.
- Includes a library, an art gallery and a bookstore.

VISITOR INFORMATION:

Admission is free. Opening hours vary.

Tube Station: Moorgate
Telephone: 020 7606 3030
Website: http://tinyurl.com/CityGuildhall

LIVERY COMPANIES

From Saxon times, craftsmen in the same trade would work near to each other. That way, they could learn their trade, keep an eye on their competitors and make sure the quality was good.

These craftsmen formed 'guilds' which made sure tradesmen kept to certain standards. Members of a guild wore a 'livery', including clothes and badges which symbolised their trade.

1066
William the Conqueror invades England.

1067
William I officially recognises the City's rights.

That's why guilds in the City are called 'livery companies'.

It wasn't easy to gain membership. First, a tradesman had to do a seven-year apprenticeship. After that, he was a 'journeyman' for a period of time. When he finally became a 'freeman', he could join a livery company.

Until the 19th century, if you wanted to ply your trade in the City, you had to be a freeman. Becoming a freeman also gave you the right to vote in local elections. Even now, if you want to hold a civic office – such as Common Councilman, Alderman or Lord Mayor – you must be a freeman.

Since about 1680, judges at the **Old Bailey** have worn wigs.

OLD BAILEY

- On top of the dome, there is a gold statue of Justice. She holds the scales of justice and a sword.

Tube Station: St Paul's
Telephone: 020 7248 3277
Website: http://www.oldbaileyonline.org

1077
William I starts building the White Tower.

1189
Henry Fitz-Ailwyn is the first Mayor of the City.

There was a great rivalry among the most powerful livery companies. In 1515, the Lord Mayor decided an 'Order of Precedence' which ranked them once and for all. The first 12 were - and are - called the 'Great Twelve'. The Livery Companies were very powerful within the City's government. They elected the Aldermen and Common Councilmen to represent them on the Court of Common Council, the City's parliament.

THE ROYAL EXCHANGE

Wealthy City merchants invested in the financial markets in Antwerp, but Thomas Gresham decided the City needed its own exchange. He built the Royal Exchange with his own money, and it soon became the centre of the financial industry. Many City institutions, including Lloyd's insurance market, have been located there.

ROYAL EXCHANGE

- Originally finished in 1571, the current building was built in 1842.

VISITOR INFORMATION:
The Royal Exchange is filled with shops and is open on weekdays.
Tube Station: Bank
Website: www.theroyalexchange.com

DID YOU KNOW? By tradition, when the monarch changes, the accession is proclaimed from the steps of the Royal Exchange.

THE GREAT PLAGUE

The City was crowded with people who lived and worked within its walls. There was no plan, just a higgledy piggledy jumble of shops, homes, workshops and other buildings. Conditions were ideal for the spread of the Great Plague of 1665!

It was really bad. We don't know for sure how many people died – maybe 100,000. Authorities didn't report all the deaths, thinking it would cause panic.

The Great Plague certainly took its toll, but the City was about to face something even worse: the Great Fire of 1666.

Opposite: The **Royal Exchange**, by E. Walker, 1852.
Published with the kind permission of the London Metropolitan Archives.

MAGNA CARTA
THE City of London shall have all the old Liberties and Customs which it hath been used to have. Moreover We will and grant, that all other Cities, Boroughs, Towns, and the

1215
John confirms the City's ancient rights.

1349
The Black Plague strikes London.

Meet Sir Thomas Gresham... Merchant
(Circa 1518 to 21 November 1579)

Sir Thomas Gresham was a merchant, member of the Mercers' company and financial wizard who advised kings and queens. He served as a diplomat, built the Royal Exchange in the City and became one of the richest men in England.

In 1551, an embarrassed King Edward VI needed help with his debt problem. Sir Thomas Gresham devised different methods to raise the value of the pound on the Antwerp exchange. As a result, within a few years the King was free of debt.

Sir Thomas Gresham designed the Royal Exchange to be a financial market. He wanted it to look like the bourse in Antwerp. So he hired Flemish craftsmen to build it and imported all the materials for its construction.

When he died, Sir Thomas Gresham left money and property to create a college where professors would give free public lectures on different academic subjects. The lectures began in 1597, and to this day, they continue!

For more details, visit www.gresham.ac.uk.

> If you look closely at the weathervane on the Royal Exchange, you'll see a grasshopper.
>
> That's the symbol for the Gresham family!

1411 to 1439
The Guildhall is built.

1422
The first Lord Mayor's Procession takes place – on the river!

THE GREAT FIRE OF LONDON

In the wee hours of 2nd September 1666, a fire started at Thomas Farriner's Bakery on Pudding Lane. Authorities woke up Thomas Bludworth, the Lord Mayor. They asked for his permission to knock down houses and prevent the fire from spreading. He told them not to bother. It was a decision that he and the City would soon regret!

By morning, the fire had spread beyond the neighbourhood and across the City. Samuel Pepys watched it from the church steeple at All Hallows by the Tower, and he also took a boat along the River Thames to survey the fire.

He reported his news to King Charles II, who asked him to order the Lord Mayor to knock down buildings and stop the fire. But it was too late. The fire was already raging across the City, destroying buildings and forcing residents to flee.

There was utter chaos. People were rushing around, trying to save their things. Samuel Pepys buried his beloved parmesan cheese in his garden to keep it safe. Authorities begged people to help fight the fire, but people were leaving the City. Even the Lord Mayor left – and he was supposed to be organising the fire-fighting!

Meet Samuel Pepys... Diarist
(23rd February 1633 to 26th May 1701)

Samuel Pepys kept a diary from 1660 to 1669, which gives us a close-up view of 17th century London. In it, he wrote about ordinary things – like what he ate for breakfast, how he slept, or who he met – but he also recorded historical events, including a day-by-day account of the Great Fire of London.

Samuel Pepys worked hard and had a talent for administration, which earned him the job as Chief Secretary of the Admiralty under King Charles II. He also served as a Member of Parliament.

Read his diary: www.pepysdiary.com.

1515
The Lord Mayor sets the order for livery companies.

1563
The Black Plague kills 17,500 people.

There was no fire brigade in those days, so King Charles II put his brother James, the Duke of York, in charge. James commanded the Royal Life Guards to create firebreaks. They used gunpowder to destroy buildings in the path of the fire, and every time the fire flared up, they fought it.

After four long days and nights, the fire was finally put out. But the City was in ruins. The Great Fire had burned over thirteen thousand houses, eighty-seven churches, and forty-four livery halls. The Royal Exchange, the Customs House, the Old Bailey, the General Letter Office and the London Gazette Newspaper office had burnt down. St Paul's Cathedral (the old one) was completely destroyed, and its lead roof had melted from the heat!

Despite the devastation, it wasn't too long before plans were under way to build a new City. And that City would be better than ever.

1566 to 1571
Sir Thomas Gresham builds the Exchange.

1571
Elizabeth I decrees it the 'Royal Exchange'.

AFTER THE GREAT FIRE

Reconstruction began immediately and within ten years most of the City was rebuilt. The City had been badly in debt even before the Great Fire, and it needed to get back to work as soon as possible!

In 1667, Parliament passed the 'Rebuilding Act'. The Act required buildings to be made of stone or brick – certainly not wood! And it also forbade buildings from overhanging streets, because that's what had helped the fire jump from building to building.

The Act also provided for a Monument to be built to commemorate the Great Fire. Sir Christopher Wren and Dr Robert Hooke were put in charge of the project. These two architects had each created a new City plan after the Great Fire, but both of their plans were rejected. Each man, however, played an important role in the reconstruction.

DID YOU KNOW?

Robert Hooke designed The Monument as a huge zenith telescope. He wanted to use it for astronomy, but horses and carts in the area caused too many vibrations.

THE MONUMENT

- Designed by Dr Robert Hooke and completed in 1677, eleven years after the Great Fire.
- It is $61\frac{1}{2}$ metres high and is located $61\frac{1}{2}$ metres from the site of Farriner's bakery where the Great Fire started.

VISITOR INFORMATION:
Cost: Adult £3 Child £1.50
Tube Station: Monument
Telephone: 020 7626 2717
Website: www.themonument.info

1638
Smithfield cattle market is established.

1660
Samuel Pepys begins his diary.

Ironically, the government put a tax on coal to pay for it all. There was even a special Fire Court to settle arguments over lost properties.

Many people had lost their homes and their possessions, and they had to find a way to pay for it all. Nobody wanted to suffer losses like that again, and that's how the modern insurance industry got its start.

In fact, the late 17th century was a very creative time. Quite a few City institutions were founded after the Great Fire.

Sir William Paterson,
Founder of the Bank of England.

THE BANK of ENGLAND

In 1694, the government needed money! Sir William Paterson decided it should have its very own banker. This bank would loan the government money to fund its projects, its investments and its wars. In exchange, the government would pay an interest rate of 8%.

Within 11 days, William Paterson raised £1,200,000 from investors, and the Bank of England was born!

BANK of ENGLAND

- Nicknamed the 'Old Lady' of Threadneedle Street.
- Originally it was the government's private banker.
- It was nationalised in 1946, and it became independent in 1997.
- The Bank issues banknotes. These are printed in Essex using 3 different printing processes.

VISITOR INFORMATION FOR THE MUSEUM:
Cost: FREE and open on weekdays.
Tube Station: Bank
Telephone: 020 7601 5545
Website: www.bankofengland.co.uk/museum

1665
The Great Plague kills up to 100,000 people.

1666
The Great Fire of London destroys 80% of the City.

Not only was the Bank of England the government's bank, it was also the "banker's bank." It loaned money to City merchants who wanted to invest in international markets. These days, the Bank of England has a different role. It decides on interest rates, issues banknotes and regulates our financial system.

THE GEORGIANS

The 18th century City was a bustling, prosperous place! Thanks to the strength of the English navy, City merchants could trade safely overseas. The Pool of London became a major port. Ships from around the world sailed up the River Thames with tea, sugar, coffee, rice, grains and other foodstuffs. These were processed by factories located in "London's Larder" on the south bank and sent across London.

The City became a place which focused on money, finance and capital. Tradesmen, especially those who worked in messy or smelly trades, moved to other areas of London, which were cheaper. After they left the City, they could ply their trades without the permission or support of a Livery Company.

Meet Sir Christopher Wren... Astronomer & Mathematician
(20th October 1632 to 25th February 1723)

Sir Christopher Wren is most famous as an architect, but he considered himself an astronomer and mathematician! He designed St Paul's Cathedral and more than fifty churches in the City.

As a child, Sir Christopher Wren enjoyed inventing and building things. Throughout his life, he remained curious about the world around him. He had wide interests and talents, including astronomy, physics, mathematics and architecture.

He was a founding member of the Royal Society, which was meant for curious people like himself.

Members of the Royal Society discussed astronomy, biology, physics and other sciences, and they performed experiments to test their theories. The Royal Society led the way for the 'Scientific Revolution' in Great Britain.

1666
Sir Christopher Wren suggests a new City plan.

1671 to 1677
Robert Hooke designs and builds The Monument.

ST PAUL's CATHEDRAL

Great Paul

- Dedicated to St Paul, who is the patron saint of the City.
- The dome weighs 64,000 tons. That's about the same weight as one hundred and fifty Boeing 747 airplanes.
- The bourdon bell, 'Great Paul', weighs $16\frac{1}{2}$ tons. Great Paul is the largest bell in Great Britain, outweighing Big Ben by 3 tons!
- Sir Christopher Wren had started redesigning St Paul's three years before the Great Fire. His proposal, to tear the building down and start from scratch, was rejected. The Great Fire, however, changed that, and he got to design the cathedral of his dreams.
- St Paul's Cathedral cost £846,214. It was funded by a special tax on coal.
- You can climb 528 steps to the top of the dome for amazing views of the City and beyond.

VISITOR INFORMATION:
There is a charge for admission.
Tube Station: St Paul's or Mansion House
Telephone: 020 7236 4128
Website: www.stpauls.co.uk

DID YOU KNOW? After the Great Fire, Sir Christopher Wren proposed a new plan for the City. It included broad straight streets to replace the narrow lanes. His plan was rejected, but more than 100 years later, it inspired the plan for Washington DC.

1694
The Bank of England is founded.

1711
The 'new' St Paul's Cathedral is completed.

Queen Victoria reigned from 1837 to 1901.

THE VICTORIANS

By the time Victoria became the queen, London had grown far beyond the boundaries of the City. People had started to move to the east and south of London.

If you were a City worker, you had all sorts of options to get to work. You could walk, ride an omnibus, take a steamer ship up the river or travel on the new, fast mode of transport: the railway!

Loads of people travelled into the City each day. About 100,000 crossed London Bridge on foot! London desperately needed a bridge to the east of London Bridge.

But there was a problem – the bridge had to allow road and river traffic to keep moving. The City's economy depended on those ships in the Pool of London.

Sir Horace Jones had a solution: A 'bascule bridge' which would allow road traffic to cross the river and which would open to let ships sail through. They built Tower Bridge, and it opened in 1894.

If Sir Horace Jones had had his way, Tower Bridge would be clad in RED BRICK!

1752
The 'new' Mansion House is finished.

1850s
The Bowler Hat becomes popular.

TOWER BRIDGE EXHIBITION

- Originally painted brown, the metalwork was painted red, white and blue for the Queen's Silver Jubilee in 1977. In 2011, the entire bridge was renovated.

VISITOR INFORMATION:
Cost: Adults £8.00 Children £3.40 Under 5s FREE
Telephone: 020 7403 3761   Tube Station: Tower Hill or Tower Gateway
Website: www.towerbridge.org.uk

Meet Sir Horace Jones... Architect
(20 May 1819 to 21 May 1887)

Sir Horace Jones was a true 'City' person. He was born there, educated there and worked there throughout his life. As City Architect from 1864 to 1887, he designed Leadenhall Market, Billingsgate Market, and Smithfield Market.

His most famous building was Tower Bridge. He designed a bascule bridge, which provided a road bridge across the Thames but still allowed boats and ships to travel on the river.

Sadly, he never saw it himself. He died before it was completed.

1875
Billingsgate Market is finished.

1886 to 1894
Tower Bridge is built.

THE TWENTIETH CENTURY

The late Victorian era and early 20th century brought innovations, such as the telephone and typewriter, which helped City workers do their jobs better. And the new London Underground railway was a convenient, quick way to travel into work.

THE BLITZ

The City was a target during both World Wars. Zeppelin raids in the first war killed 650 people. In the second war, the City endured night after night of the Blitz.

When it was over, the City was devastated. Enemy action had destroyed 17 livery halls, 18 churches and countless homes, warehouses and factories. More than 500 people had died. Many people, especially those not involved in financial services, had moved out of the City for good. The City would have to rebuild – again.

DID YOU KNOW? A group of 300 volunteers, called St Paul's Fire Watch, looked after St Paul's Cathedral during the Blitz.

1907
The Old Bailey is completed.

1940s
The Blitz destroys large parts of the City.

THE CITY TODAY

Visit the City now, and you'll see construction everywhere. There are more cranes than you can count. They are building skyscrapers which dominate the skyline. With all this development, London's most ancient area will also be its most modern!

Nine hundred years ago, the tallest building in London was the White Tower. At a staggering height of 27 metres, it was a symbol of King William's power.

If William were alive today, he might be overwhelmed to see buildings, such as the Gherkin (180 metres), the Heron Tower (230 metres) and the Broadgate Tower (161 metres), which dwarf his Norman castle. He would certainly understand that these skyscrapers symbolise the wealth and prosperity of the modern City.

The best thing about all this construction is: whenever they're planning to build something new, they bring in archaeologists to excavate the site.

And those archaeologists always seem to dig up something which gives us a fascinating insight into the City's past.

Our book is just the beginning... go discover the City for yourself!

2004
The 'Gherkin' is completed.

2010 to 2011
Children at Randal Cremer Primary School create this book!

THE FUTURE!

FURTHER RESOURCES

Museums & Libraries

Museum of London
150 London Wall, London EC2Y 5HN
Telephone: 020 7001 9844   www.museumoflondon.org.uk

London Metropolitan Archives
40 Northampton Road, London EC1R 0HB
Telephone: 020 7332 3820   www.cityoflondon.gov.uk/lma

Guildhall Library & Bookshop
5 Aldermanbury, City of London EC2V 7HH
Telephone: 020 7332 1858
Guildhall Library: www.cityoflondon.gov.uk/libraries
Collage Image Library: http://collage.cityoflondon.gov.uk/collage/app

Guy Fox Resources
These publications are available FREE upon request from
www.guyfox.org.uk/ContactUs.php.

The Monument: Facts & Figures (poster)

Tower Bridge Mini-Magazine

Explore the City with Guy Fox (map)

Download these FREE teaching resources, available as PDFs, from
www.guyfox.org.uk/OurArchives.php.

The Monument Teachers Kit (PDF)

Tower Bridge Exhibition Teachers Kit (PDF)

If you enjoyed this book, you'll love these other publications created by the Guy Fox team.

LIVERY QUIZZERY

Match each Guy Fox to the Livery Company which would fit him:

Baker   Fishmonger   Fletcher

Mercer   Wax Chandler   Woolman

Spectacle Maker

WHO AM I?

Solve the riddles, then unscramble the circled letters to reveal a City occupation.

1. I was a merchant and financial advisor. It was my idea to build the Royal Exchange in 1566.

___ ___ ___ ___ ___ ___

2. I was the leader of the Iceni tribe. The Romans treated us badly, so I led an attack on London.

___ ___ ___ ___ ___ ___ ___ ___

3. I watched the Great Fire of London from the top of a church steeple, and I wrote about it in my diary.

___ ___ ___ ___

4. I was the City architect from 1864 to 1887. I designed Tower Bridge, but I died before they finished building it.

___ ___ ___ ___ ___

5. After the Great Fire, I designed The Monument. I wanted to use it as a huge telescope!

___ ___ ___ ___ ___

The occupation is: ◯◯◯◯◯◯

SPOT THE CHANGES!

The Lord Mayor's Coach is different to the coach on the opposite page. How many differences can you spot?

CITY OF LONDON WORD FIND

```
B A N S V N R O L S M A S A M P E P Y S
O M A N S I O N H O U S E O B N D R R T
U D P E R C K Y M S R N O L L I T Z O P
D R R O B E R T H O O K E B T O R W B A
I A Z C H R I S T O P H E R W R E N E U
C O L Z U O B T N E M U N O M R H I R L
C G R E A T F I R E U M Y C O H O K T S
A N B N K L V M E L L S E F R V O R H C
L L A H D L I U G A H T L M P I T E V A
G O G E N B L I T Z R O I O S K N H O T
H N Z R A O A N I O N L A R N I S G K H
E D T O M W N I E D D W B N I N M O E E
G E I B S L D D O M O B D U A G E R T D
W F U R O E W N L N L R L M X S O O H R
R N O G A R D O O S I G O R O K E I K A
T O W F D N U L R G U R O Y A M D R O L
B A N K O F E N G L A N D N R E W A L L
```

☑ Bank of England ☐ Great Fire ☐ Mansion House ☐ Romans
☐ Blitz ☐ Guildhall ☐ Monument ☐ Sam Pepys
☐ Boudicca ☐ Londinium ☐ Old Bailey ☐ St Pauls Cathedral
☐ Bowler ☐ Lord Mayor ☐ Robert Hooke ☐ Tower of London
☐ Christopher Wren ☐ Vikings
☐ Dragon ☐ Wall
☐ Gherkin

Shape-by-Shape
HOW TO DRAW ST PAUL's CATHEDRAL

When you first look at St Paul's Cathedral, it seems very difficult to draw. But if you look a bit more closely, you will see that St Paul's is made up of simple shapes. All you have to do is draw the right shapes in the right place! If you can draw the following shapes, you can draw St Paul's Cathedral:

Half-circle   Square   Tall Rectangle   Wide Rectangle   Circle   Triangle   Mushroom

Drawing St Paul's is a big challenge. But just like any big challenge, if you take your time and break it into small parts, you can do it!

And by the way, if you can draw St Paul's, you can draw just about ANYTHING!

1 Draw a half-circle for the dome and add 4 wide rectangles underneath. Add a circle and a square to both sides.

2 Draw 2 wide rectangles and a triangle. Then draw 8 tall rectangles with 'mushrooms' on top and squares underneath. Add 2 wide rectangles underneath to make a plinth.

3 Add some lines for detail and a triangle within your first triangle.

4 Add more tall rectangles with 'mushrooms' on top and 2 wide rectangles underneath. Draw a square on each side.

5 At the bottom, draw a square on the left side and 3 rectangles. Then add two tall rectangles with 'mushrooms' on top. Add 2 rectangles and a wide rectangle. Then do the same on the right side.

6 On the left, add 4 squares & 4 tall rectangles with 'mushrooms' on top. Add 2 wide rectangles. Then do the same on the right side.

7 On the left, draw a square with a bubbly rectangle on top and 3 little squares on top of that. Add some tall rectangles with mushrooms on the top. Top it off with rectangles, a square and a half-circle. Do the same on the right side.

8 Add the cross and the statues, which are mostly squares and circles. Feel free to be inventive!

9 Add the other details — including circles, half-circles, squares and rectangles. This is where the building really starts to come to life!

10 Add more details to the building, including a squiggly line in the middle triangle. That's the frieze!

11 Add the lines on the dome and squares for the 'dentilles'. Once you've added these and a few details, you're finished!

And here it is! A drawing of St Paul's Cathedral!

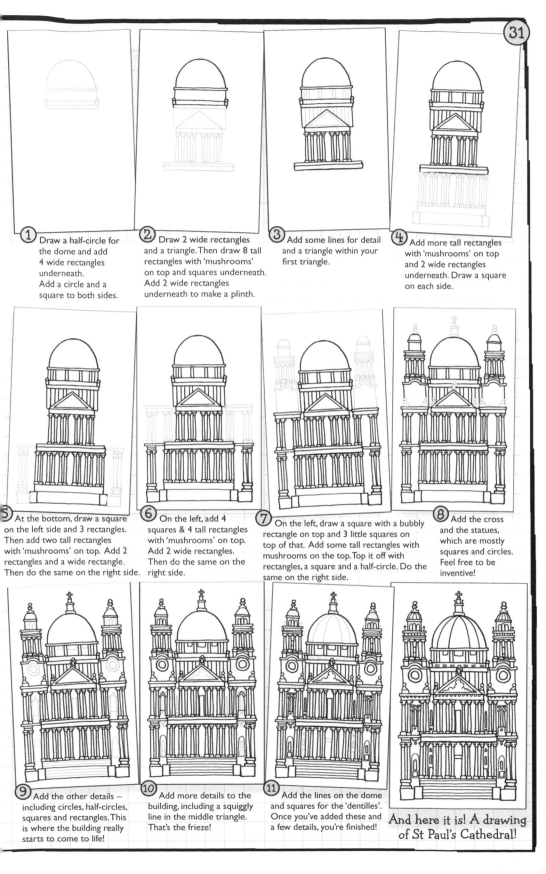

ANSWERS

Step-by-Step How to Draw St Paul's Cathedral:
If you'd like more help with your drawing, you can download a free copy of
'How to Draw St Paul's Cathedral' from www.guyfox.org.uk.

CITY OF LONDON WORD FIND

LIVERY QUIZZERY

1 Wax Chandler
2 Spectacle Maker
3 Fletcher
4 Woolman
5 Mercer
6 Baker
7 Fishmonger

WHO AM I?

1) Thomas Gresham
2) Boudicca
3) Samuel Pepys
4) Horace Jones
5) Robert Hooke
The occupation is
BANKER!

GUY FOX: 13-Waving with opposite side hand,
14-Colour of feather.

There are 14 changes.

HORSE: 1-Front leg, 2-Strap, 3-Reins, 4-Colour of tail.

DRIVER: 5-Colour of feather, 6-Expression on face,
7-Number of hands, 8-Colour of gloves.

COACH: 9-Number of Tassels, 10-Colour of wheel hub,
11-Knight's head orientation, 12-Number of spokes.

SPOT THE CHANGES!

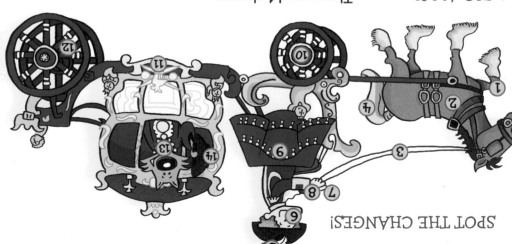

Guy Fox 'City' Stickers

Banker

Lord Mayor

Spectacle Maker

Fishmonger

Mercer

Wax Chandler

The Lord Mayor's Coach

 WARNING! Choking Hazard.
Not suitable for children under 36 months due to small parts.